Promoting Positive Self-Esteem in Children

Presented by Bridging The Gap Training

Terry J. Walker, M.A.

Life on Purpose Publishing

NEW CASTLE, DELAWARE

Promoting Positive Self-Esteem in Children/ Terry J. Walker, M.A. -- 1st ed.

ISBN 978-1-7336950-6-0

Dedication

This book is dedicated to two of the strongest people I know, my mom and dad. Thank you for always being there to support me and to push me to succeed in my endeavors. Although I made mistakes, you helped me to work through them and to never give up. You supported me in times of crisis and were there in times of celebration. You helped prepare me for adulthood by instilling the love, courage, confidence, and integrity that it would take to overcome life's obstacles. Thank you for loving me and being there for me. I love you.

Bridging the Gap Training was developed to provide a unified point of connection towards improving communication, understanding, and mindfulness between people and/or groups of people to achieve successful results.

I wish you love and light on your journey as we all work together towards Bridging the Gap.

Namaste' my friend,
- Terry

Contents

Parents and educators need to fill a child's bucket of self-esteem so high that the rest of the world cannot poke enough holes to drain it dry.

–ALVIN PRICE

Before You Begin

YOU ARE LIKELY here because you love your child and are willing to do your part to create a successful, thoughtful, confident, young person who displays positive self-esteem. Parents, grandparents, guardians, teachers, early child educators who interact with children on a regular basis play a large role in their development. The expression, "it takes a village" has always been true, but never truer than today.

Enlisting all the adults who are part of the village to agree on expectations, responsibilities and consequences is no small task. Getting them to follow through is even more difficult. Unfortunately, any weak links on this team can undermine the long-term goal—a responsible and emotionally healthy young adult.

Hopefully, this information will allow you to share your insights and skills with the team to empower them to join forces with you.

The influence of family in the first few years of life is undeniably the most important part in creating a solid foundation for positive self-esteem. Regardless of how the family is identified, the most critical task is working together in the best interest of the child.

Setting limits and rules is the beginning of creating consistent expectations, accountability, and positive outcomes for your child. These rules make it much easier to set limits for them in school, as pre-teens, and in their teen years.

"It is easier to build strong, children than to repair broken adults." -Frederick Douglas

Truer words have never been spoken. As children begin to grow, what happens in daycare, preschool, and elementary school become the next big influences towards their development of self-esteem. Since confidence is the outcome we seek, their educational environment is a crucial piece of the puzzle.

Many moving parts lead to self-confidence—which should not be confused with self-importance. Self-esteem begins and ends with clarity, focus, intentions, accountability, inspired action, and achieving successful outcomes.

After working on the front lines with families, educators, children, and adolescents, I often asked myself, what are we missing? What is happening with our children during those early years? It was then I began to research, study, and develop *Bridging the Gap, An Educator's Guide* and *Bridging the Gap, A Parent's Guide*.

Bridging the Gap between parents and educators was developed for the self-enhancement and socialization of our children. If you are a parent, a guardian a grandparent or an early child educator, this program is developed especially for you.

Bridging the Gap training provides education, tools, and techniques that you will be able to implement immediately.

Many have asked: what is your definition of bridging the gap? My response: "to provide a unified point of connection towards improving communication, understanding, and mindfulness between people and/or groups of people in an effort to achieve successful results." In other words, let us bridge the gap from where you are to where you want to be.

As you learn more about self-esteem, you will read an example story that exemplifies many important principles. You will learn about Ben and Maria, siblings from an intact family with different parenting experiences which leads to different early outcomes.

Ben's experience shows that even those who have learning disabilities can still become confident, successful young people with the right team of adults supporting them. Likewise, Maria's story shows that regardless of aptitude, her confidence required more creative awareness and understanding.

The end of this guide has some self-reflection questions for you as a parent or educator. You may find it helpful to write down your responses to these questions before you begin reading and then again after you finish. As you learn more, you may experience some change in your original responses.

In essence, even as a parent, we are all teachers as we help our children to grow, develop, and become successful.

As an educator, you spend a tremendous amount of time with children and you too play a major role in the life and development of a child. I tip my hat to you as a parent or educator and thank you for all your hard work, dedication, and desire towards inspiring our kids to be the best they can be, and for empowering them to become emotionally healthy and self-confident young people!

> *"A teacher affects eternity: he/she can never tell where his/her influence stops." -Henry Adams*

CHAPTER 1

What is Self-Esteem?

SELF-ESTEEM IS BASED on our belief in our own worth—it is the confidence we have in ourselves. It is a subjective assessment of ourselves that may change over time, and possibly even day to day. The term *self-esteem* is often used interchangeably with terms such as self-worth, self-confidence, and self-regard.

People who have a positive self-esteem are usually more self-assured, and therefore often willing to take more chances that lead to positive results. They are less concerned about making mistakes and looking foolish to others.

Those with low self-esteem may second-guess themselves, feel somehow "less than," and be overly concerned about what other people think of them.

How Do We Develop Self-Esteem?

Like many things, self-esteem is the result of our interactions with people whose opinions shape our core personality. Usually, the opinions and interactions of authority figures such as parents, teachers and others are important to our developing sense of self – essentially who we are as a person.

We see ourselves as others see us, especially as children. Those who receive the message that they are accepted, able, and worthy — either verbally or otherwise — are more likely to view themselves in that way. Unfortunately, the opposite is true, as well.

It is common to recognize patterns of low self-esteem that impacts someone's life. Oftentimes, it is rooted in childhood experiences and learned from the behavior of others — meaning it can begin early and impact all areas of the person's life.

CHAPTER 2

The Great Self-Esteem Experiment

IN THE '70s, parenting experts and others came up with the idea that we should collectively support the development of positive self-esteem by using praise for the slightest accomplishment—merely showing up, for instance—and downplaying, if not totally ignoring any type of failure. This experiment included changing the grading system in schools from passing or failing to comments such as: "needs improvement, satisfactory, or exceeds expectations." Tee-ball and other sports became cooperative instead of collaborative. Rather than competition, we all focused on cooperation.

Of course, this led to the advent of the participation ribbon which rewarded those who did not put in as much effort as those who dedicated themselves to excellence. The outcome was a huge failure. While the focus on praise for effort is valid, and fostering cooperation and collaboration are critical, removing expectations and accountability from the equation really complicates things. Providing rewards for just showing up without implementation of effort to achieve results can lead to an exaggerated sense of accomplishment.

Showing up should be mandatory, not necessarily rewarded. It reminds me of the old saying which still holds true today, "We must get up, dress up, and show up." By itself, showing up does not accomplish the goal. One must also put in the work and the time.

Consider homework, for example. Your child brings their book bag home, which may be an accomplishment for some, but a given for most. They have the book in the bag along with a homework assignment. They take the information out of the bag, and in essence, they have shown up. However, do they begin working on the assignment through completion, or do they sit there doodling, playing on their phone, and wasting time?

Which behavior is the accomplishment?

- Bring books home
- Complete homework assignments

As parents and educators, what are the goals and expectations that we set for our children? On the other hand, what are the goals we are setting for ourselves as adults and educators? Are the goals clearly set so there is minimal confusion? Are we allowing for excuses for ourselves, and even making excuses for our children?

For example, do we call the teacher and make an excuse for the child when he or she falls short, so the child does not experience the natural and logical consequences of their behavior? Think about it:

- What does a child learn when we lie on their behalf to protect them from a consequence?
- What message does it send when we run interference between our kids and their consequences?
- Is this the behavior you exhibit, and in turn are teaching your child?
- What happens when we do not allow our children to deal with their failures?
- How do kids learn coping skills if they never experience failure or negative consequences?
- How do people learn responsibility without expectations?

In the great self-esteem experiment, the goal was to protect kids from negative consequences so they would feel good about themselves. The thinking at the time was that negative consequences, or failure, would damage their self-esteem; they would see themselves as lacking, failures, or some equivalent.

In effect, we were trying to build a strong ego—and we did but it resulted in a sense of self-importance without the confidence that comes with accomplishment. In fact, we inadvertently created a generation of adults who have difficulty accepting any type of critical feedback, responsibility or accountability and expect to be rewarded for just *showing up*.

THE STORY OF BEN AND MARIA

Siblings with vastly different experiences

Ben has always struggled in school. He has learning problems in math and spelling but excels in sports. He is on the varsity basketball team, which requires him to keep at least a C average in his classes. His desire to play basketball keeps him motivated in class. The teamwork between Ben and his teachers, coaches, and parents are instrumental to his success both on and off the court. Although Ben has trouble with academics, his teachers love him. He is a kind, respectful teenager and tries to do his best in school. Ben's mom is a strong advocate, but she has clear expectations and boundaries about his schoolwork.

Ben knows that he can ask for help anytime he needs it. He also knows that Mom will not make excuses for him if he doesn't turn in his homework or study for tests. The consequences for failure are clear—no basketball.

Ben's coach is invested in both his academic and sports success. He encourages Ben to do his best both on and off the court. When he fails or makes mistakes, Coach and Mom help him process the experience and learn what he can from it.

Ben is so motivated by basketball that he gives 100 percent in the classroom. However, at times, he makes failing grades in math.

When Ben's favorite aunt died, he had difficulty sleeping and focusing on his classes. He kept up his homework but failed two tests in math. The week before Homecoming, Ben received an F on his report card. It would have been easy to give him a pass under the circumstances since losing his favorite aunt was difficult for Ben.

Although basketball was important to him and he was experiencing a significant loss, he accepted responsibility for making a failing grade. Ben understood that he would need to sit out until mid-term grades were reported.

Meanwhile, he dressed out for games and sat on the bench. He never missed practice and continued to support the team. Ben also asked to do extra credit work in math, which helped raise his GPA.

Ben's mom realized basketball was the motivation for him keeping up his grades. In turn, his interest in basketball was largely responsible for how he managed to feel confident despite his academic challenges.

She also knew that not following through with these consequences would be failing Ben. **The delicate balance between succeeding in sports and accountability in schoolwork contributed to his positive self-esteem.**

As you see, it took a *team* of adults working together in collaboration. Everyone had Ben's best interest at heart to help him feel productive, confident, and successful.

Maria, Ben's sister, was an entirely different story.

Maria was the younger child and only girl. From a young age, she was treated as a princess by her doting father and grandparents. She was gifted academically and bored in school by the end of first grade. She had no interest in sports, art, or other extracurricular activities. However, she had an innate love for animals and could not wait to get home every day to play with her dog and cat, Marley and Mickey. The only way to persuade her to do homework was by removing the pets from her study area until she finished her work.

Maria's parents were *not* in agreement on parenting styles. Dad left it up to Mom to deal with Ben, but often undermined her efforts with Maria. Although her Mom tried to hold Maria accountable for homework and chores, her Dad allowed her to play with the pets during study time.

The consequences of not caring for Marley were clear, Maria would clean up any messes if she neglected to take the dog out for walks and potty breaks, as this was their agreement when they adopted her. However, Dad readily cleaned up the mess when Mom was not around.

Despite her academic gifts, Maria did not feel good about school. She reported feeling lost in a pool of students and overachievers. Her primary desire was to become a dog groomer after graduation. The thought of continuing higher education was of no interest to her. It was difficult to get her up in the mornings, and oftentimes, she would be late for school.

When Maria received detention for excessive tardiness, her dad tried to intervene and persuade the vice-principal to reconsider. This worked the first time, but within the next month, it happened again. When Maria refused to accept responsibility for detention, the vice-principal added an extra hour with the understanding that she would be suspended for three days if she did not serve detention as assigned.

Maria's grades began to slip when her aunt died. And she stopped hanging out with her friends. Everyone was concerned about her, including her dad and grandparents. The loss of her aunt was significant and brought everything else to the surface.

When they began family therapy, the first challenges identified were low self-esteem and lack of parental agreement on rules, consequences, and follow through. The therapist helped the parents work on their part of the issue, and enlisted Ben to help Maria accept responsibility for her choices by providing positive support and spending more time talking with her.

Maria learned to think before acting. **Volunteering for the local rescue became both a reward and a way to reinforce her success.** Over time, Maria became more engaged in school and started a weekly community service project between her school and the rescue organization. Her grades improved as part of the agreement for managing the community service project. She also made friends with many of the volunteers. She blossomed with the success of the program and gained more self-confidence.

Although both children were in the same family, they exhibited different interests, and unique skills and abilities. The keys were to recognize what inspired the children, as well as what provided consistency, support, and communication between parents, educators, and other contributing adults. Everyone worked together toward establishing creative ways to set clear goals, provide positive support, and create awareness of the emotional guidance system toward helping both children establish confidence and feelings of success.

As you see, it took more than just *showing up*.

CHAPTER 3

Steps to Positive Self-Esteem

HOW CAN YOU help your child develop positive self-esteem? Self-esteem comes from within. It is not something we can give our children; however, **we can foster it by teaching them the skills they need to gain confidence.** Part of that process entails allowing them the freedom to make positive choices and to understand failure.

Self-esteem comes from within. It is not something we can give our children; however, **we can foster it by teaching them the skills they need to gain confidence.** Part of that process entails allowing them the freedom to make positive choices and to understand failure.

Many of us have a fear of failure, and because of that fear, we sabotage ourselves from taking chances, from learning, from growth, and from success and development.

Understanding and learning from failure is part of the growth process. For those who have illusions of control over their kids, this can be difficult. Many of us attempt to control our emotions, our growth, our situations, and our children. We spend a great deal of time and energy attempting to control outcomes, and by doing so, we often sabotage ourselves and our children. I am sure you have heard the saying: *the tighter we try to hold onto or control someone or something, the more out of control the situation becomes.*

Step 1: Communicate with Clarity and Positivity

Setting realistic, clear objectives and goals lead to accountability. Be clear and ensure you both understand and agree on the objectives. **If needed,**

spell it out step-by-step. This is part of teaching children what you want them to do, rather than reprimanding them for doing it wrong.

Here are a couple of examples.

> *"Each day, I want you to bring your books and assignments home for your classes. After you finish your snack, do your homework. When I get home from work, I will review your assignments for the next day. If they are not complete, you will not have phone, TV, or computer time until everything is complete. Any questions?"*

> *"For every day that your assigned chores are completed by 7 p.m., you will earn $2. If the chores are not completed, you will not receive an allowance for that day."*

If needed, outline specifically what needs to be done for a chore to be considered complete. For example, "make your bed, pick up everything lying on the floor, fold and put away clothes."

Write it down, make a check list, and allow your child to participate. Make it colorful, creative, and fun.

Keep in mind that once the goals are met, many of us get caught up in taking them for granted rather than providing positive acknowledgment and appreciation for a job well done.

When dealing with choices and consequences, sometimes we get so focused on right and wrong, good and bad, and implementing a consequence that we forget about the reward. Keep in mind that rewards are of the greatest importance when a child is doing well, exhibiting consistency, and showing improvement. Start perceiving the glass as half full instead of half empty. Recognize the good and expand on it to promote more positive responses and positive outcomes. As discussed earlier, positive reinforcement builds confidence for a child who is doing well.

As adults, if we consistently try to do well, and never receive positive reinforcement for our actions, we will likely stop trying. We may even feel as though we are being taken for granted. No one likes to feel as though the job they are doing is not appreciated by a family member, a colleague, or a boss. Keep this scenario in mind when your child is doing what they have been asked. It is your opportunity to take notice and provide positive accolades and/or small celebrations.

If we only get attention or reinforcement for negative behaviors and actions, then we learn to behave negatively in order to receive some type of attention. This is called negative attention seeking or negative reinforcement. To counter negative reinforcement, it is especially important to remain aware that the child is making efforts and doing what is asked of them. It is the parent's and/or educator's responsibility to implement positive reinforcement for positive behaviors.

I would like to interject a segment from my book, *The Resume' of Life*:

> *"Like any parent, we do not always agree with the choices our kids make, but I have come to recognize we cannot be with them 24/7 to make their choices for them. What we can do is model, teach, love, and respect them. But we cannot hold onto, control, or force them to be a certain way. As with*

energy, when you apply force, you will receive counterforce. Help them find, strengthen, and maintain their internal sense of knowing. Help them to recognize those negative influences and forces that will come along during their journey. You are there to teach, to support, and help them to work through their growing and learning processes. They need to be allowed to find their unique expression and build upon it. Teach them, model positivity for them, help them, support them, but most of all: love and accept them for who they are."

Step 2: Everyone on the Same Page

Clear rules and expectations should be agreed upon by all adults, including grandparents, educators, and sitters.

Promoting inconsistency can lead to issues such as manipulation, insecurity, and stress while decreasing accountability, confidence, and responsible behaviors. One of the most important aspects in working with children is effective, consistent communication within the family and with educators.

My grandfather used to tell me "the right hand needs to know what the left hand is doing." To be effective, parents and educators need to communicate how the child is doing in class, educationally, socially, and developmentally. If the educators do not inform parents the child is doing well or the child is having difficulty dealing with others or obtaining necessary skills, how can we be effective in helping the child? You can bet that the child will not inform the parent what took place in school.

Do you remember this question, "What did you learn (or do) in school today?" The response was usually, *"nothing."* This is the primary reason it is so important for parents and educators to communicate and work together to maintain consistency in helping a child learn and grow both emotionally and educationally.

On the other hand, if there are concerns at home such as health, grief, loss, financial stressors, the educator may be of benefit by helping provide a more supportive, safe environment for the child. When parents and educators effectively communicate with each other, they inspire continuity, understanding, trust, and consistency—along with eliminating confusion, misunderstanding and uncertainty.

Step 3: Provide Consistency and Accountability

To feel successful and confident, we must be willing to be accountable for our choices and actions. If you make it clear that homework will be checked when you get home from work, check the homework and be consistent. Hold up your end of the bargain and help them to understand the importance of accountability and priorities. You cannot expect your child to do their part, if you are not accountable for what you say and do.

As a child, many of us heard the phrase, *"Do as I say, not as I do."* If you were told that as a child, you probably remember how it made you feel.

As an adult, if you are always complaining and blaming others for your struggles rather than being accountable for your actions, how do you expect your children to behave? If you are inconsistent in following the parameters you put in place, you are sending a message that the issue is not important, and there is no need to follow through with your responsibilities. In essence, you are inadvertently teaching your child that you are not accountable.

The result is a mixed message, and as we know, children learn by watching. The child may take advantage of these lessons by blaming others, slacking off, or not following through with their responsibilities.

When there is a ballgame or another extracurricular activity after school, be definitive about when homework will be done. Provide clear communication in advance whenever possible. "Do your homework ahead of time tonight since you'll be late getting home tomorrow after the game."

Any time we can be proactive in getting something completed ahead of time, the better off we are. This stops the negative habit of procrastination which injects more stress upon us.

Step 4: Allow Them to Experience the Natural Consequences That Arise from Their Choices

You must be willing to let them fail and understand the consequences that may come from that failure. This is where most people stop nodding in agreement.

This requires that your self-esteem can withstand any criticism or negative feedback from teachers, family, friends, and others. It is a time in which you become aware that you have a limited amount of control over another human, even your child.

During this journey of life, we all encounter negative feedback. We also make poor choices, and we need to be held accountable for our actions. We all experience failure, and we need to learn how to overcome these obstacles and understand how we can learn from them, rather than allowing them to define us. This is how we grow, and this is how we learn.

"Success is not final; failure is not fatal; it is the **courage to continue** *that counts." -Winston Churchill*

With any luck, they may only have to fail once or just a few times before they understand the lesson at hand. For example, your child will begin to realize that it is their responsibility to do what is required for school, and that you will not protect them from the consequences of their actions and choices.

Here are few examples of language you can use:

It's time for bed. I see that your homework is not complete. You will have to go to school tomorrow and explain to the teacher that you did not complete your homework.

If you receive detention for your behavior, you'll have to serve it. If you get a failing grade, you will need to work harder to recover.

The coach may drop you from the roster if you don't pass the class. In turn, you may have to repeat the class in summer school.

If you have established a more positive awareness of your own behaviors, accountability, and communication skills, it stands to reason your child will mirror your behavior and begin to *do as you do*.

This section should provide both parents and educators with ideas toward implementing appropriate consequences for behaviors. It also will help instill a rewards system. It is our responsibility as adults and role models to help children grasp the concept of right and wrong and to learn that certain behaviors will either have consequences or rewards. It also helps to instill accountability for our actions.

How you choose to reinforce a child's behavior makes a difference. It is also our responsibility to establish a reward system and consistently reward or reinforce positive behavior. I want to caution you to not get caught up in the *consequence game* and forget about the rewards. We can discipline a child in several ways which help a child realize and practice accountability so he or she will not make the same mistakes. In turn, provide feedback that helps our children grow and thrive. As adults, we do not have to be controlling or demanding to get our point across to a child.

We can stand firm and continue to remain consistent and positive, along with everyone communicating effectively.

Step 5: Learning from our Failures and Shortcomings

"Failure should be our teacher, not our undertaker. It is a delay, not a defeat. It is a temporary detour, not a dead-end street."-William A. Ward

Failing is most helpful when we learn something from it, and often, it can be our greatest teacher. We all must learn to live with our decisions and actions, or inaction. Failure can help us to grow, to improve and to continue to move forward if we are willing to recognize what we are to learn from this experience, and what can we do to improve and make a better choice next time.

Events *or experiences happen every day. Ultimately our **response** to those events will determine the **outcome.***

This is also an excellent time to teach and process with the child. Ask them what they learned from the experience and what they can do to make it better if the event occurs again.

However, you may want to avoid asking this when the tension is high. Allow some time for emotions to subside and find a teachable moment to discuss it. Talk about how you or the child could handle this situation differently in the future. Do not be afraid to apologize for your errors or anger. This becomes a teachable moment for both you and the child.

Be aware that sometimes we all make the wrong choice and sometimes we make them more than once. At some point, we realize if we continue to make the same choice, we are also choosing the consequences that go with it.

We all make choices that are not always the in our best interest, even though we know what the consequences or likely outcome will be. Learn to let go and always love them while sticking to your standards, even when you are disappointed, and they are upset. Try asking something like, "Are you ready to talk about what happened today and what you can do differently next time?"

If not, do not push it. Allow for some time to pass and feelings to subside while maintaining your composure you can then say, "Let me know when you're ready to talk about it."

Effective processing with the child:

- Encourage the child to identify improved choices should a similar event arise.
- Facilitate a potential scenario with the child and help him or her process different choices along with the potential outcomes for those choices.

This facilitation process helps the child understand that when faced with certain events, he or she can learn to process potential outcomes prior to the choice being made. This encourages the ability to think before acting and encourages coping, problem-solving, and decision-making skills.

Step 6: Encourage Good Behavior and Avoid Reinforcing Bad Behavior

Catch them being good is a phrase that cannot be overstated. **When your kids perform actions you want to see more of, thank them and show appreciation for what they are doing.**

Tell them you appreciate them and be descriptive about what you appreciate. "I appreciate it when your chores are done early, and we can relax, or play a game or go for a bike ride after dinner."

Reinforce their efforts even when they miss the mark. "I know you tried your best on the math test. Maybe your teacher can offer some guidance on what you missed. What do you feel you need to improve? We could speak with your teacher together about some additional help or credit work in the subject."

Keep in mind that asking for help is not a sign of weakness or failure. We all need help and support every now and then.

However, be aware that you do not inadvertently lower the expectations. For example, the expectation might be that the chores are done before bed. Acknowledge it with a simple "Thank you for cleaning your room today." While this shows acknowledgement and appreciation, it does not lessen the expectation. Hopefully, you are already reinforcing this behavior, along with a weekly allowance or positive reward.

Completing the chores early and without stress or constant reminders is something you want to praise and reinforce—going beyond the minimum.

Everyone has feelings, and at an early age, children are gaining a sense of awareness and are establishing their own self-esteem and socialization skills. Children who live in a positive home environment and attend school or daycare in an environment filled with consistency and positive reinforcement, are more likely to exhibit healthy skills and positive choices.

On the other hand, children who live in a negative environment and experience anger, stress, abuse, and inconsistency are more likely to act out to obtain negative attention.

Many studies have shown that emotional well-being influences educational performance, learning and development. Studies also revealed that children between the ages of 3 – 10 who experience extreme emotional stress present a greater risk of poor adult mental health to include lower brain activity in the areas that are linked to motivation, positive moods, and depression.

Conversely, children who have a positive support system and consistency from one or more caring adults are more inclined to overcome traumatic events more readily.

Oftentimes, we see people who categorize children in one of two ways: *good* or *bad*. You have heard the saying that the "squeaky wheel gets the grease." *Good kids* usually receive positive reinforcement, while *bad kids* usually receive negative reinforcement. In both circumstances, the child receives some type of reinforcement. As we know, children love attention and want to be reinforced, noticed, and validated.

Unfortunately, the opposite will ring true as the primary attention some children receive is negatively reinforced. Many children may live in a negative, highly stressed environment. Hence, to obtain some type of attention and to feel noticed, these children feel they must act out.

As adults, we too want to be recognized for our efforts and accomplishments. **We all need to feel that we matter.** Everyone appreciates positive reinforcement from others, whether it be our partner, boss, colleague, parent, or teacher.

Children are the same way. They want to be loved, appreciated, and accepted. They want praise, attention, recognition, and rewards for their efforts and actions. When we are recognized or validated for our efforts, our self-esteem increases and encourages us to want to do more.

Step 7: Provide Opportunities for Your Child to Succeed

Allow children to make choices from an early age, within reason. "You need to put on a coat before leaving for school. Do you want to wear the red or green one?" You have given them a choice but have not given them the option to leave without a coat. It is a safe way to teach decision making at an early age. This has provided the child to think about which coat to wear and gain excitement for the opportunity to choose which one they prefer.

As they get older, the choices become riskier, but that is part of the developmental cycle. Those who begin making decisions at an early age will develop more confidence, and therefore, will be more likely to make improved choices later. Allowing and providing for children to make reasonable choices at an early age builds confidence.

Step 8: Love Them Anyway

Learn to detach from the outcome. Do what you can to uphold your responsibility to your children and accept that you cannot control the situation. We all make errors in judgment, but again, we all can learn from it rather than to remain in it. We must keep moving forward to learn and to grow.

If not, we will continue to repeat the same cycle and receive the same or similar outcomes.

As adults, we do not appreciate when someone constantly reminds us about a mistake from our past. We also know it is difficult to move forward if we keep looking back. Keep this thought in mind as we continue to teach and encourage our children.

With each choice, there will likely be a consequence or a reward. The primary goal is to make the best decisions we can when an event arises. When we have an opportunity to contemplate and weigh out our choices ahead of time, we increase our chances for a better outcome. By doing so, this allows children to learn how to weigh out the options and potential outcomes prior to making a choice.

Gentle reminder—to separate the behavior from the child we should keep this thought and comment in mind; I might not like what you did, or the choice you made, but **I love you**.

Step 9: Understand and Implement Positive Affirmations and Positive Self Talk

Affirm: to validate and confirm. To state as a fact; to offer support or encouragement.

Affirmations are a wonderful way to improve and grow self-esteem whether for yourself or your child. Affirmations are powerful and begin with two especially important words: *I am.* What you choose to place after those words creates your reality.

By integrating affirmations into our thoughts and words, we make positive changes and improve our confidence. Begin positive self-talk with words such as: *I am, I can, and I will.*

For example:

I am loving; I am happy; I am worthy; I am successful; I am smart, I am beautiful, I am kind, I am trusting, etc.

Use positive, descriptive words and say them numerous times a day. Make it fun and creative.

Once you begin to change your thoughts to positive self-talk and implement affirmations, you will start to feel, believe, and experience more confidence.

Affirmation Game

Start with the letter A. Come up with as many positive words beginning with the letter A as possible, and begin utilizing these positive words after I am. For example:

> *I am... abundant; I am... able; I am... aligning. Move on to the letter B and so on. You can do this while looking in the mirror, as a game with your child, driving down the road, or taking a walk. Take turns with your child.*

This exercise allows both you and your child to be more creative in your thoughts by utilizing positive words that you can begin to incorporate into your thoughts and vocabulary.

As you practice this exercise, you will find yourself speaking to someone and using these words while speaking and potentially helping someone else to be inspired by your encouragement and support.

You can also begin acting with the phrases: *I can, and I will.* Example:

> **I am** smart and capable. **I can** pass my test. **I will** pass my test by committing to study at least 30 minutes each day during the week prior to the test.

> **I am** athletic and **I can** make the team. **I will** practice my free throws for one hour each day for the next two weeks so **I will** be prepared for try outs on the team.

> **I am** a great piano player. **I can** qualify for the upcoming recital. **I will** prepare for the recital by practicing one hour each day for the next month so **I will** be prepared for the tryouts.

> Gentle reminder—I can, and I will are specific action steps. Utilize them as a goal by adding a specified time frame along with what you are going to do to help you achieve the goal. By setting

and obtaining our goals, we build confidence, accountability, and improve decision making skills.

Once the goal has been achieved, be sure to provide positive reinforcement or a special celebratory event.

Gentle reminder — if a specific goal is not achieved, you will need to help the child process the disappointment or outcome. This encourages the child to not give up, but to become accountable for what they can do to continue to grow and improve.

Step 10: Implementing the Emotional Guidance System

What is the Emotional Guidance System and why is it important?

Our emotions and instincts help guide us toward or away from certain situations. Emotions help us understand, connect, and improve communication with others, along with connecting with our true selves. They also alert us when something is wrong, or potentially dangerous, and they help influence our choices and decisions.

Are we living life on Auto Pilot?

Today, we pass our co-workers in the hall, and one asks, "How are you today?" Our *auto pilot response* is usually, fine, or okay, and we both keep walking in opposite directions. You likely feel the person that asked, "How you were doing," may not really care if you were having a horrible day, or if you were having an exceptionally great day.

How are you? has become an *auto pilot* question. On the other hand, by answering this question with words such as *fine, alright,* or *okay* has also become an *auto pilot* response.

The point is that we do not take the time to see how someone really does feel, nor do we take the time to inventory our own feelings. Our questions and responses have become automatic with no real thought as to how we truly feel.

With the implementation of social media, we now use emojis of happy, sad, surprised, angry. We give a like, love, sad, angry, all with one click of a mouse. We may or may not leave a comment as we continue to scroll down the timeline providing little or no regard to our true feelings, and possibly minimal thought to our friend who posted the information.

It appears we may be living on auto pilot and have turned our emotional guidance system into a convenient drive-through store speaking words or clicking emojis that are quick, painless, and require minimal thought or response.

If we are unconscious or unable to inventory our own feelings, then how can we expect our children to be more conscious of their feelings?

The words: *fine, good, bad, alright, and okay* are <u>not</u> feelings or emotions.

Even with technology today, somehow, we have forgotten how to inventory and express our true feelings.

The words *good, bad, fine,* and *okay* have become our *auto pilot* terms at the convenient drive through store.

Below is a brief exercise from the "Bridging the Gap" books and trainings that I ask parents or educators to utilize at home/school and make a game out of it. This feeling activity inspires identification of feelings with the expressions on the feeling faces. It allows children to identify what they are feeling and the event that transpired to cause them to feel that way.

1. Everyone sits down and turns off distractions such as the television and phones.
2. Take a few minutes to review the feelings sheet provided on page 71.
3. Identify an event of the day and identify how it made you feel by utilizing a feeling word.
4. Discuss the event or experience that caused the feeling. Did the event make you angry, happy, grateful, sad, stressed, afraid, etc.?
5. Explain how they dealt with the identified feeling. For example, did they laugh, grateful, cry, hit or throw something.
6. If they were unable to deal with the feeling appropriately, help them to come up with

    a. improved alternatives to be able to express their feelings appropriately.

    b. If they expressed their feelings appropriately, provide praise.

    c. Remember to help facilitate and allow the other child(ren) to interact, provide praise, and/or help provide each other with alternatives and solutions.

This promotes active listening, effective communication, and positive interaction along with inspiring creative, problem solving skills.

For example, when helping to process the event and feeling:

- Identify the feeling-- such as happy.
- Describe the event that transpired to allow them to feel happy
- What did they do to show their happiness?
- Did it make them laugh, want to play, or dance or tell someone?
- Identify the feeling of mad or angry.
- Describe the event that made them mad or angry?

- Did they cry, stomp around, slam a door, throw something, hit or kick someone?
- Identify more appropriate ways to handle the anger.
- If in a classroom setting, allow for the other children to help the child identify alternative ways to appropriately express the anger. Also, if the other children witnessed the outburst, allow them to identify and process their feelings about the experience.

These exercises initiate the child(ren) to think, communicate, and learn more about him or herself. It should also help the child(ren) understand and deal with their feelings more appropriately, along with enhancing communication and improved coping skills.

Gentle reminder—anger is a feeling and is an important part of our emotional guidance system. It is okay to be angry. It is how a person deals with anger that becomes a problem. The parent or educator can help the child brainstorm ideas on how to handle feelings more appropriately and then begin to help him or her to practice and role-play some of those ideas.

Role-playing is a valuable tool which provides children an opportunity to see for themselves (mirror), how they may act and are seen in certain situations.

Not only did the parents/educators take a few minutes out of their day, they created a time of learning, bonding, and open communication. It only takes a few minutes to provide quality—not necessarily quantity—time. By implementing these processes, you have incorporated communication, coping skills, established trust and awareness, and fostered understanding of the emotional guidance system.

As an early childhood educator, you can do the same with your class. Take a few minutes and allow the children to discuss their feelings. Allow them to discuss how a specific event made them feel. Help them to learn to communicate with each other by using feeling terms.

I have trained early child educators on these feelings exercises to utilize in class and help them provide the information to the families. They have returned to tell me that not only are they seeing positive changes in the classroom, but the parents are recognizing it at home as well. Remember, as with anything, it must be practiced and used consistently.

Should you be interested in more information: You will find more in *Bridging the Gap, An Educators Guide, Bridging the Gap, A Parent's Guide,* and/or we will discuss the emotional guidance system more in depth in Bridging the Gap Training Workshops.

Potential repercussions from ignoring our emotional guidance system:

- Increased risk of alcohol/drugs and other risky behaviors
- May become more aggressive and present bullying behaviors
- Increased stress and anxiety
- Withdrawal from school, work, friends and family, interests, and hobbies
- Difficulty focusing

- Increased risk of heart disease, diabetes, cancer, depression, and memory impairment
- Inability to make decisions and lack of effective coping skills
- Low self-esteem and confidence
- Psychosomatic symptoms

CHAPTER 4

Bridging the Gap Training

BRIDGING THE GAP Training is the foundation to work with your child during the early years to establish a positive sense of self-worth, confidence, communication, and coping skills.

It is not intended as a be all, end all program or training to perfect parenting or teaching, but it has been developed with inspiring and empowering information for you as a parent, guardian, or educator to be more creative in establishing a healthy, lasting, and trusting bond with your child(ren).

Each person responds differently to different structures and dynamics. The important concept to remember is that you are the parent, the teacher, and the role model for your child. Children learn by watching. How you cope and respond to certain situations is how your child will learn and mimic your behaviors.

Behavior is learned, and whether you are the parent, guardian, or educator, your role in a child's life is essential.

If you want your child to learn to accept responsibility for his or her actions, it begins with you exhibiting consistent behaviors as the role model. If you want respect, you must respect yourself and provide respect to others. The days of "*do as I say, not as I do*" need to become a statement of the past for you and your family.

I recognize that people and families are different, and I hope you take what you can, be creative, and use the information to your advantage and growth.

The work force is changing rapidly and so must society and our role in it. Government and corporations have placed more stress on people to work harder and possibly longer hours just to remain employed. Families and family dynamics have gone by the wayside in the adults' effort to maintain a home and pay bills. We find ourselves in a world of working all the time and always striving but never arriving. We go to work, come home, put dinner on the table and everyone goes their separate ways. We may spend our evening upset from the day's events or complaining about the day, and we allow it to consume our evening as well.

Today, with COVID-19 we are under even more stress. School is inconsistent. Many of us are forced to work from home while attempting to oversee our child's online learning. We may be experiencing issues with childcare, concerns about our health and the health of our family. Along with this, we may also be experiencing job loss and financial issues.

Many of us are operating under a great deal of fear and stress, and our children are experiencing this fear and stress as well. Now is the time to get back to nurturing our families and ourselves. Otherwise, we will continue to remain as a hamster on a wheel, always running to keep up and never really accomplishing anything.

We lose our sense of self in this dynamic, and we lose our sense of family. Stress is taking over our lives as a parent, educator, employer, and with our children.

Social media has become more prevalent and is used as an outlet or pastime for our children and ourselves. However, it can also become detrimental to the entire family. We witness anger and blame along with children being exposed to unhealthy and possibly incomplete or inaccurate information on the Internet or through their friends.

Bullying is now a huge factor in schools, and violence is becoming rampant both in schools and through social media. We have started to live in fear for our children to go to school. School is supposed to be a safe place for our children to grow and to learn without the worry of being bullied, beaten, or even killed.

We must learn to take back our lives and our families and become more aware of what is going on around us. Otherwise, we are allowing outside negative influences and forces to run our lives and the lives of our families.

Whether those outside forces or influences come in the form of job dissatisfaction, social media, violent video games, sex, drugs, etc., we must become aware of these influences and work to educate ourselves about them.

You have heard the statement: knowledge is power. Now is the time we must become more aware of our lives, thoughts, habits, and actions. How are you representing yourself? Are you caught up in fear, stress, anxiety, and worry? How are you helping you children adjust to all the change and stress with COVID19? We must be creative, positive, proactive, and aware of what is happening around us. All the while, being strong and confident enough to help our children have a bright and productive future.

This involves understanding our family dynamics by building trust, confidence, and maintaining an open line of communication within the family and with our educators. It means we need to incorporate positive self-development, understand our thoughts, habits, feelings, and behaviors, so we create the energy to help nurture and develop our families.

Setting the Tone for Our Day— Breaking the Snooze Button Habit

I WOULD BE remiss - if I did not add this information for you.

When we first awaken, our brain and body is the calmest, freshest, and most aware that it will be for entire day.

Ask yourself this question: when I first wake up in the morning what do I think about and what are my first actions? Once you have answered this question, my question to you is: Was your answer anything remotely based on the following?

- Lie in bed and begin to worry and/or dread all the things I must get done
- Push the *snooze button* on the clock and roll over to attempt to sleep a little longer
- Jump up immediately and start rushing around trying to get things done
- Pushed the *snooze button* one too many times and now feel aggravated or frustrated and running behind
- Immediately begin looking at phone or computer to check emails, social media, etc.

If any of these examples or something similar are how you begin your day, then that is the tone you have set for your day. These are habits. If these are the habits you exhibit, then likely your day will continue with *feelings* such as stress, anxiety, frantic, dread, chaos, frustration, exhaustion, along with thoughts or statements such as: I don't have time; I'm too busy; I'm too tired. **These are the moments and habits that define you. How you react or respond will determine your outcome.**

We know our children learn from us, and if we are thinking, acting, and living in stress, chaos, dread, frustration, agitation, and anxiety, then it stands to reason our children pick up on these habits, feelings, and stressors as well.

As I mentioned earlier, when you first awaken is the calmest time of the day in which your brain and body is most relaxed and open to creativity, focus, and growth.

What can we do to improve setting the tone for our day, and in turn, help our children do the same?

- Break the Snooze Button Habit! Be willing to stop pushing the snooze button both literally and figuratively.

- Set an intention to create a positive day with positive outcomes.

- Take a few moments when you first awaken to establish gratitude or appreciation.
- Identify your habits and become aware of what habits are hindering your growth.

Positive Habits to Incorporate

- Lie there for a few moments and define things to be grateful for such as:
    o Health
    o Safety
    o A new day
    o Family
    o Home
- Define positive feelings of gratitude and what you can do to **create** your day rather than dread your day.
- Raise your energy and set your intention for a productive, positive day rather than a negative, stressful day.
- Take time to listen to something positive and motivating that lifts your mood:
    o Podcast

- o Motivational Video
- o Music
- Journal your thoughts or goals.
- Read something positive or motivating.
- Think and speak positive affirmations. Incorporate affirmation games with your kids while getting ready for your day.
- Take time to do some deep breathing, stretching, or exercise. This helps to awaken the body and increases your energy for the day.
- Meditate. Take a few minutes to sit quietly and go within to listen, to center yourself, and to visualize positive outcomes.
- Create a priority list for your day which improves your time management.
- At the end of the day, take time to be grateful for what you accomplished that day. Have an end of the day discussion of gratitude and sharing time with your kids.

After reading these suggestions, some of our first thoughts may be: I don't have time for this.

As a matter of fact, "I don't have time," could also be considered a quick *drive-through* phrase just like, "how are you doing," wouldn't you agree? Not only that, but you have once again pushed the snooze button.

For example, the habit of procrastination will lead to feelings of stress, exhaustion, and anxiety, and of course, never enough time to get things done. My question for you is, "How has that been working out for you?"

One of my favorite statements is, *"If you continue to do what you've always done, you will continue to receive what you've always gotten."* In fact, if you make the effort to stop pushing the *snooze button* of procrastination and replace it with a new habit to get up 30-60 minutes earlier and implement some of the above listed habits, you will begin to:

- Feel better—emotionally, physically, mentally
- Improve your confidence
- Increase your energy and productivity throughout your day
- Decrease feelings of stress, anxiety, and exhaustion

- Increase appreciation for yourself and those around you
- Set a positive example for your children and help them to establish productive habits

My guess is that if you have made it this far, then you are looking to make productive, positive changes for yourself and your family. You have the choice. In fact, the choice has always been yours to make.

As you set the tone for each day, you have the choice to make it positive and productive or chaotic and stressful.

A gentle reminder: these are the moments and habits that define you. How you react or respond will determine the outcome.

The Self-Esteem Ladder

Expectations leads to accountability.

Accountability leads to responsibility.

Responsibility leads to choices.

Choices lead to rewards or consequences.

Consequences lead to critical thinking.

Critical thinking leads to taking more calculated risks.

Taking risks leads to success and failure.

Success and failure lead to learning.

Learning leads to growth.

Growth leads to confidence.

Confidence leads to achieving goals

CHAPTER 7

The Self-Esteem Boosters

- Positive affirmations: begin positive self-talk with the words: I am, I can, I will. For example, I am loving; I am happy; I am worthy; I am successful. Use positive feeling words and say them numerous times a day. Make it fun, and once you change your thoughts to positive affirmations, you will begin to feel, believe, and see the difference in yourself. In turn, you will be much more effective in teaching and role modeling it to your children and/or class-room.

- Reinforce successful behaviors.
- Do not be critical and too quick to criticize.
- Do not ignore or overlook successful behaviors or accomplishments.
- Celebrate successful behaviors with joy, praise, and encouragement.
- Help the child to express his or her thoughts and feelings.
- Realize that everyone makes mistakes, even adults. Help the child to learn and grow from mistakes. Do not belittle or degrade them.
- Talk it through and remain open and calm. When negative events occur, encourage the child to process and overcome the stressful feelings.
- When we as adults make mistakes and our child recognizes our error, we should be willing to accept responsibility for our actions. We cannot teach responsibility and

accountability to our children if we are unwilling to do it for ourselves.

- Implement and maintain an open line of communication

Kind Attention

One simple habit that we can incorporate immediately is *kind attention.* Kindness provides us with courage to look at the part of ourselves that we may not want to see. Kindness also bathes us with dopamine which activates the learning centers of the brain and provides us the resources we need to change. Incorporating true and lasting transformation requires utilizing kind attention.

How can I begin practicing kind attention? Learn to say you love yourself and allow for kindness to yourself daily. Some of us may feel that saying, "I love you, (your name)" to yourself is too difficult. If so, start with an easier statement such as saying, "good morning, (your name)". As you say it, place your hand over your heart and take a couple of deep cleansing breaths. Allow for and feel the peace and calmness come over your body.

Once you have practiced the good morning mantra, add *"Good morning, I love you, (your name).* Continue to place your hand over your heart, feel your heartbeat, and take three deep cleansing breaths. As you release your breath, count to 4 in your mind so it becomes a slow relaxing release. Incorporate this practice into your daily morning routine when you first awaken each day. Begin to add new statements and identify what you are grateful for. As you begin implementing kinder, more positive thoughts and statements, you will begin to improve your energy, thoughts, confidence, and recognize what you are practicing is growing stronger.

The Feelings
Game Sheet

Self-Reflection

CONSIDER THESE SELF-REFLECTION questions in your endeavor to promote positive self-esteem in your children:

- How often do you provide opportunities for your child to learn by allowing them to make decisions on their own?
- How well do you uphold your responsibilities by being clear about expectations and consequences, following through, and working together with other adults?
- How do you process mistakes and failures and help your children learn and grow?

- Do you separate the misdeed from the child?
- In what ways do you show that you appreciate their efforts when they do their best?
- How do you reinforce good behavior and choices?
- Do you allow your kids to experience negative consequences for choices and behavior?
- Do you process choices, possibilities, and consequences with your child prior to the choice being made to help enhance critical thinking and processing skills?
- Do you accept responsibility for your actions or mistakes and process what you could have done better with your child?
- What habits and behaviors are you role modeling?

Be honest with yourself as this information is here to help you. You did not acquire this information if you were not interested in developing your skills, and in turn, empowering your child.

As mentioned earlier, knowledge is power, and our greatest aspiration is to learn, grow and improve. In essence, when we do this, we inspire others to do the same, and that includes our children.

After all, you and your children deserve it!

Your Invitation to Bridging the Gap Training

I'd like to take this opportunity to invite you to learn more about the Bridging the Gap program. After working as a Program Director and Therapist in inpatient treatment, program development, along with providing family therapy, I wrote my two Bridging the Gap guides.

Since that time, I have developed *Bridging the Gap Training workshops* which provide the opportunity to work directly with parents and educators. The goal of *Bridging the Gap* is to help us all work together for the self enhancement, socialization, and positive development of our children.

Consider the following information as mentioned in a previous chapter. Studies have shown:

- Children who experience extreme **stress** between the ages of 3 – 10 pose a higher risk of poor adult mental health to include lower brain activity in the areas that are linked to motivation, positive moods, and depression.

- However, children who have a **healthy support system** from one or more caring adults can overcome traumatic events more readily.

As I stated before, with COVID-19, uncertainty, fear, confusion, and increased stress on our families and educators trickles down to our children. Study after study has shown how the effects of stress, fear, abuse and change in family dynamics such as divorce, death, and financial loss, have a profound effect on our children's learning, socialization, self-esteem, and development. With ongoing continued stress, our children are more likely to have:

- Reduced impulse control
- Difficulty building healthy, trusting relationships
- Poor coping and communication skills
- Difficulty processing feelings
- Higher incidence of unhealthy behaviors such as substance abuse, promiscuity and engaging in other risky behaviors

- All of this can also lead to physical health issues such as: obesity, diabetes, heart disease and suicidal ideations

Bridging the Gap training has been developed to inspire effective communication between parents and educators for the social enhancement of our children.

It is the gap between feeling confused, stressed, and alone as we deal with all this change, not only in the workforce, but in our families and in the education system.

Conversely, it is the bridge for parents and educators to begin working together for the benefit of our children towards enhancing your child's self-worth, confidence, positive development, and socialization skills. Below are a few common themes I found when working with kids and families:

- Difficulty in establishing healthy relationships
- Trust issues being a way of life
- Poor communication skills serve as a root cause of problems

- Instances of anger, stress, anxiety, and depression serve as a child's way of reaching out

Questions to Consider:

- Do we feel it is "uncool" to question your kids or discuss feelings?
- What impact is social media playing in our lives today?
- How can do we effectively communicate and express our feelings?
- What effects are online/intermittent education having on the socialization and self-esteem of our children?
- What emotional effect is COVID-19 having on us, our jobs, our kids, and our health?
- Are parents and educators communicating about our kids with progress updates or concerns?
- How are we dealing with stress during this time of change and confusion?

Strategies and Techniques on How We Will Effectively Begin to Bridge the Gap:

- What to do and what to expect along stages of development
- Role modeling and understanding how fear, stress, and anger shut down opportunities for growth and learning
- Implement clear communication, along with the art of active listening
- How to discuss feelings and implement the emotional guidance system
- Encourage decision making and problem-solving skills
- Learn what stress does to the body and mind, along with techniques to overcome stressful situations for both us as adults and for our children.
- Mindfulness techniques to include the awareness of thoughts, behaviors, habits, actions, meditation, and the power of affirmations.
- Power of role-play and feedback.

- Build healthy, trusting relationships

I trust this information has empowered you with positive, creative ideas and insights that you will implement in your home or classroom.

I hope you inform your friends and colleagues about *Bridging the Gap Training*. I look forward to meeting and working with you as we all begin working together towards *bridging the gap*.

You can find out more about the training workshops at: www.bridgingthegaptraining.com

I wish you and your family all the best on your journey to continued growth, love, and light.

Namaste' my friend

- Terry

About the Author

Terry J. Walker, M.A.

TRAINER, SUCCESS COACH, Consultant, Motivational Speaker, Radio Host and Author, Terry J. Walker has dedicated the past 30 years to educating, training, inspiring and motivating others to improve their lives.

Terry is a member of Champion Mindset Team and has shared the stage with such great speakers as Les Brown, Nick Bollettieri, Bernard Hiller, and Brian Tracy.

Terry has a Master of Arts Degree in Educational Psychology and Counseling. She is a Success Coach, and a Jack Canfield Success Principles Trainer. She has over 10 years of experience in the medical sales and customer service industry and over 15 years of experience in counseling and program development in the mental health field working with children, adolescents, and families.

Terry is the author of 3 educational, empowering books:

- *The Resume´ of Life* — using her personal experiences as a backdrop, Terry has provided a guide to assist in understanding the correlation between career and life resume. The book provides a greater sense of clarity and focus on how your choices and decisions have led you here, and what changes can be made to enhance objectives and goals to inspire both personal and professional development.

- *Bridging the Gap, An Educator's Guide* — An empowering guide for early child educators to improve their awareness towards helping children identify feelings, enhance self-esteem and socialization skills, improve communication, and establish healthy boundaries and relationships.

- *Bridging the Gap, A Parent's Guide* – An inspiring guide for parents and educators to bridge the gap towards boosting communication, mindfulness, and improving quality time with their children.

All her books and trainings are designed to empower, illuminate, and simplify, while boosting communication, mindfulness, leadership, cultivating relationships and achieving overall greater success in both personal and professional development.

Terry is the founder of *Bridging the Gap Training*, a series of motivational trainings providing a unified point of connection towards improving communication, awareness, and mindfulness between people and/or groups of people in effort to achieve successful results.

She is also the creator of the *Soul Stretching Success Principles*, a coaching program providing the tools, ideas and techniques to help others grow, transform, and generate powerful changes toward creating the successful lives we are meant to live.

Based in the greater Nashville area, Terry is the Owner and Founder of Inspire and Motivate, IAM, LLC – The company provides impactful training and coaching on leadership, mindfulness, communication, success skills, stress management, and discovering your true potential towards creating a successful life of overall personal and professional development. The acronym I AM- two powerful words for what you choose to put after them creates your reality.

To find out more or invite Terry to your conference, virtually or in person, please visit:

- www.iamterryjwalker.com
- www.bridgingthegaptraining.com
- email: terry@iamterryjwalker.com

Made in the USA
Coppell, TX
25 March 2022

75541263R00059